Curbing Anger,
Spreading Love

Bhikkhu Visuddhācāra is a Malaysian Buddhist monk. He was a journalist before he became a monk in 1987. He was ordained by the Myanmar meditation master Sayadaw U Pandita from whom he learnt insight *(vipassanā)* and loving-kindness *(mettā)* meditation. He presently resides in Penang, Malaysia.

Curbing Anger, Spreading Love

Bhikkhu Visuddhācāra

With illustrations by
Hor Tuck Loon

Buddhist Publication Society
Kandy • Sri Lanka

Published in 1997

BUDDHIST PUBLICATION SOCIETY
P.O. Box 61
54, Sangharaja Mawatha
Kandy, Sri Lanka

First published in 1992 by
MALAYSIAN BUDDHIST MEDITATION CENTRE

ISBN 955-24-0123-2

Book layout and design by
    LIM HOCK ENG,
    SUKHI HOTU SDN. BHD.
    42V, Jalan Matang Kuching
    11500 Air Itam, Penang, Malaysia

Printed in Sri Lanka by
    KARUNARATNE & SONS LTD.
    647, Kularatne Mawatha
    Colombo 10

To my preceptor,
the Venerable Sayadaw U Panditabhivamsa,
and to all my teachers who taught me
the theory and practice
of the Dhamma.

To all my Dhamma friends and benefactors,
known and unknown,
without whose compassion and support,
I would not have been able to become a monk
or to remain one until today.

May the merits accruing from this work
be to the weal and happiness
of all my teachers and benefactors
and all sentient beings.

May all beings be well and happy.

ACKNOWLEDGEMENTS

I am indebted to Venerable Bhikkhu Bodhi, President of BPS Sri Lanka, for editing and improving on my original work and finally publishing it. To Hor Tuck Loon: without your fine illustrations, this book would have been all the poorer. To Venerable Suceta: thanks for helping and encouraging me to write when I was plagued with self-doubts. To Lim Hock Eng: for completing the layout and design for this edited version. To Hor Kwei On: for the many hours he spent on the design and layout of the first edition. To Sayadaw U Pandita: for showing me the path, guiding me in the practice of insight and lovingkindness meditation. Without him, this book would not have taken birth. To Venerable Sujiva, Sayadaw U Jatila, Sayadaw U Lakkhana, and all my other teachers and benefactors: thank you for your guidance, support and kindness.

CONTENTS

SPEW IT OUT!

pew out the venom of hatred from your heart—that hatred which is poisoning and choking all that is good and beautiful in you. Why would you want to have anything to do with this venom? Spew it out, throw it all out, every bit of it. Throwing it out will be good for you.

Then fill the heart with the soothing balm of loving-kindness. Let it permeate every pore of your being. Soaked like a sponge with tenderness, reach out with a mind of pure love. Let every being who comes within the ambit of your presence feel the magic aura of your goodness, such that when they take their leave, they depart fortified with more confidence and courage to face this often hard and cruel world.

Hark! Listen, my friends. Like a lamp, small but steadily glowing, we can ignite many other lamps and lo! perhaps we may yet drive out the black night of despair, dispel the murk of delusion, and bring back the pure light of wisdom and love.

(A state that) starts with madness,
and ends with regret.

- Abraham Hasdai

ANGER
A DESTRUCTIVE EMOTION

 o you get angry? Of course, all of us undeniably do. Now and then we may get irritated, annoyed, peeved. We get angry or exasperated with this person or that person for this reason or that reason. There are many things and conditions which can cause us to be vexed and annoyed. Usually we get frustrated and angry when we do not get our way. We want things done in a certain way and when they are not done in that way, we get angry, we get mad. Sometimes we may be expecting something to come about (such as a pay raise), and when it does not happen, we get upset and angry. Then there are people who provoke or offend us. They have a knack of getting on our nerves.

In fact there is no shortage of conditions that can spark off our anger. If we were to observe our reactions and responses in the course of a normal day, we would find many occasions when we lost our cool or were on the verge of losing it. Anger shows in the way we speak and gesticulate, the changes in our facial expressions, the irritation in our voice, the way we snap and raise our voice. And when we lose further control, we might start to shout, yell, kick, slam a door, bang the table, slam down the phone or even physically strike or assault somebody. In extreme cases, people have been known to kill out of anger, or while in the grip of rage, drop dead from a heart attack!

Our anger may vary in intensity. Some people are hot-tempered; they blow up easily. Others are said to have a mild disposition; they appear to be always cool and calm. Some nurse grudges long after their anger has passed while others may be more forgiving. Whatever it is, the fact remains that all of us do get angry, the difference being only in the intensity and frequency of the emotion. For even the most mild of persons can show signs of vexation and irritation when his patience is over-taxed, or when he is under too much pressure.

Should we get angry? Is there such a thing as righteous anger? Is it all right to get angry and yell at people, to lose our cool and blow our top? Has anger become a way of life among people in the world? Have we taken it for granted and come to accept it as something natural and unavoidable? When we read today's newspapers, we would find no shortage of anger and hatred in our planet. Reading about all the fighting and continuous warfare in various parts of the world, do we pause to wonder why people cannot live together peacefully as brothers and sisters? Why are we so unforgiving, so brutal, so merciless? Why do some kill innocent people to get what they want? Why do countries compete to make nuclear weapons that can destroy everybody in the world? Why is there so much fear and distrust?

Anger starts from our heart, just as love does. It is our firm belief that anger is an evil which should be banned completely from our hearts and minds. It is a destructive emotion that has caused much misery in the world and in our lives. It begins from the mind and it is at the source, the mind, that it must be checked and eliminated. The pre-amble to the UNESCO Constitution, too, states: "Since war begins in the minds of men, it is in the minds of men that the defences of peace must be built." Santideva in his *Bodhicaryavatara* (The Entrance to the Life of Enlightenment), wrote: "How many evil men could I kill? Their number is boundless as the sky. But if the thought of anger is killed, all enemies are killed."

Anger makes our life miserable. If we continue to accept anger and make no great effort to curb it, we will continue to live turbulent lives. Every time we become vexed, annoyed, angry, we begin to burn men-tally. This burning feeling increases with the intensity of the anger. The stronger the anger, the stronger we burn. It is a very painful sensation. You can observe it for yourself. The next time you are vexed or angry, look at the state of your mind and heart, and see for yourself the pain and suffering you are undergoing because of that anger.

Anger is an unwholesome state of mind. The Buddha never allowed for anger of any kind. In Buddhism there is no such thing as righteous anger. All anger, even of the subtlest level or briefest duration, is bad. It is like a poison to the mind. Thus the Buddha exhorted us to return love for anger: "Hatred never ceases through hatred. Only through love does it cease. This is an ancient and ageless law." On another occa-sion he said: "Conquer the angry man by love."

Emphasizing his point with a simile, the Buddha said that even if a robber were to use a saw to cut off our legs and hands, we should not give vent to even the slightest bit of anger. If we were to become even a little angry or annoyed, we would not be following his teaching. Instead, the Buddha exhorted us to radiate love towards the tormentor. "For thus you ought to train yourself," he said. "Undisturbed shall our mind remain, no evil words shall escape our lips, friendly and full of sympathy shall we remain, with heart full of love, free from any hidden malice. And those persons (the robber or robbers cutting off our limbs) shall we penetrate with loving thoughts, wide, deep, boundless, free from anger and hatred."

Such was the Buddha's perfection in love. Even as a *bodhisatta* (a Buddha-to-be), he had in countless previous lives undergone torture and death without harbouring an iota of hate or anger towards his tormentors. And in his last life as the Buddha he was always cool and serene. Never did he lose his tranquillity and equanimity. When the mad elephant, Nalagiri, charged at him, the Buddha was able to subdue the animal by radiating loving-kindness towards it. The Buddha's missionary work of forty-five years, with little rest, was an exemplification of compassion and love.

The Buddha, of course, is not the only teacher who preaches love and compassion. All great teachers do so. Jesus Christ said: "Love thy neighbour as thyself." "If somebody strikes you on the right cheek you should turn and offer him the other cheek." Mahatma Gandhi, the great advocate of non-violence, said: "If blood be shed, let it be our blood. Cultivate the quiet courage of dying without killing. For a man lives by his readiness to die, if need be, at the hands of his brother, never by killing him." This brings to mind the story of a monk who was threatened by a fearsome general. "Don't you know," roared the general, "I am the kind of person who could kill you without even batting an eye."

The monk replied: "And I, sir, am the kind of person who could be killed without batting an eye." Faced by such a stout heart, the general walked off without harming the monk.

Besides being poison to our mind, anger and hatred are also a danger to our physical health. Medical science has confirmed that anger and other unhealthy emotions can contribute to bodily disease. When we are angry our body discharges certain chemicals that can upset our physical well-being. If such behaviour is habitual, it can in the long run lead to various ailments, such as stomach ulcers, indigestion, constipation, high blood pressure, heart trouble and even cancer.

On the other hand, a calm and peaceful state of mind is conducive to both mental and physical well-being. We will be healthier, happier and live more fulfilling lives. Some of the chronic ailments that may be troubling us, such as indigestion, may clear up. Other illnesses may also be averted. The serenity and radiance of a tranquil mind will be reflected in our physical features and complexion. Wherever we go we will be liked and loved by all. Nobody likes to mix with an angry person or with one who gets angry easily. A boss who is always frowning or shouting at his employees is shunned and disliked. His workers will not think twice of leaving when an opportunity arises. But the boss who is always smiling, kind and helpful, who never or rarely loses his temper, is loved and cherished. For such a boss, some employees would not leave even for a better salary elsewhere.

Furthermore, your virtues will have an influence on all who come into contact with you. You will be an example for others to follow. In what better and more sincere way can we change the world than by setting an example? Yes, by changing ourselves and setting an example,

People make up the world.
If we change ourselves
we change the world.

we are actually contributing positively to a better world. For just consider: The world is made up of people; people make up the world. If you change the people, you are changing the world. And you start with yourself. After all, are you also not one of the people in the world? Thus, when you change yourself, you have changed the world in the sense that there is one less anger-prone person in the world. If more people change themselves, then the world will be changed to the extent of the number of people who have changed. With more peace-loving people around, the strife and turmoil in the world will decrease.

Recognizing the evil of anger and the harm it can do to ourselves and others, let us dispel anger and radiate loving-kindness. Let us be tender and patient, gentle and helpful. Let us not be harsh. Let us not confuse, bewilder and perplex others. Look around and see: there is enough sorrow in the world already. Let us not add to it. Let us instead be a source of comfort and peace; let us be like a light unto the world so that all who come within the circle of our influence can walk more safely and happily.

Making the determination to curb anger and spread love is a first step. The next question is: How do we go about doing it? It is not easy to control our anger when it arises. It takes a lot of effort and skill to keep anger under rein. Therefore, in the following pages we will discuss ways and techniques of curbing anger. It mainly involves mindfulness (*sati*) and wise reflection (*yoniso manasikāra*). By being mindful we can nip the anger in the bud, even as it is about to arise. And applying wise reflection on the many reasons why we should not get angry will remind us and convince us that it is desirable to evict the anger promptly from our mind, to drop it, so to speak, like a hot brick. In the third section, we will present the meditation on loving-kindness *(mettā-bhā-vanā)*, one of the best "antidotes" for anger. We believe that if the reader considers the many reasons why we should not get angry, he would not want to get angry at all, and the next time anger arises he would want to drop it straightaway. And together with the cultivation of mindfulness *(sati)* and loving-kindness *(mettā)*, he should be able to put the demon of anger to rest.

May all beings be happy. May they root out anger and hatred from their hearts and become the embodiment of great love, wisdom and compassion.

Put away anger, abandon pride,

overcome every attachment,

cling not to mind and body

and thus be free from sorrow.

- Buddha, Dhammapada 221

ANTIDOTES
FOR ANGER

 First rule: Mindfulness *(sati)* is the first and best guard against anger and all unwholesome states of mind. What is mindfulness? It is presence of mind, awareness, knowing clearly what is happening right at the very moment of its occurrence. Thus, the moment anger arises, one must apply mindfulness. One must quickly take cognizance of the arising of anger in oneself. One must note, acknowledge or say mentally to oneself: "Ah! There is anger in me. Anger is arising in me." Or, one can just note tersely as "anger, anger." Or, if one does not wish to label, one can just be aware of the presence of anger without labelling it.

When one notes it thus, the anger is spotted and its presence acknowledged. Just this mere act of knowing is helpful in checking the anger. Why? Because whenever anger arises, it usually overwhelms us even before we know it! It clouds our reason, impairs our better judgement, takes control of our mind. At that time, we are hardly aware of our own anger. Instead, we are already consumed by it, responding and

MINDFULNESS
is the first rule.

reacting to it. Our facial expression changes and we start to snap, gesticulate or even yell at somebody. Mindfulness checks all this. It prevents the anger from overwhelming us. It institutes a much needed presence of mind. Just the mere act of knowing helps to cool down the flames of wrath. Instead of responding or reacting to the anger, we watch it. We watch the hot feeling, the emotion. And in that watching, in that observation, the anger can subside. First it will weaken and then it may vanish.

Furthermore, when we observe the anger, we no longer pay attention to the person, object or condition that is arousing our anger. Instead, we are looking inward at our own state of mind, at the presence of the emotion of anger. Logically, when our focus of attention shifts from the object (i.e. the cause) of our anger to the pure awareness of anger itself, as an emotion, the anger will weaken. For if we had continued to focus on the object (such as the person) we were angry with, the anger would have naturally increased. But under the glare of mindfulness, anger cannot intensify. It is checked, and with continued noting, it weakens further and finally subsides.

And the wonderful thing too is that the anger subsides without any suppression or force. You need not grit your teeth, clench your fist or use sheer mental force to overcome the anger. Instead, as you note, the anger just weakens and dissolves by itself. This is the miracle of mindfulness. It can be especially clear in an intensive meditation retreat when the meditator's mindfulness is so sharp that it can knock out the anger or any other unwholesome state of mind by the mere act of noting.

Another benefit of mindfulness is that it allows us to pause and make the right decision or response. When we note and take cognizance of the anger, we will not be carried away by the emotion. The pause gives us time to reflect and decide on a wise course of action. In that interval, we have an opportunity to exercise what the Buddha called *yoniso manasikāra*, wise reflection or proper consideration. So if the anger did not subside completely through our initial noting, then we can reflect in various ways on the evil and disadvantages of anger. In the course of reflection, our anger will naturally weaken, and as we become more and more convinced that anger is undesirable, the anger will subside. A desire *not* to be angry will arise and eventually vanquish the anger.

Thus, the first rule is to exercise mindfulness. If you make it a habit to be mindful of significant changes in your mental states, your mind will become so sharp that you can "catch" the anger the moment it arises. You can feel and know that anger is emerging and thereby nip it in the bud, eliminate it well before it can show on your face or in your actions. That's the magic of mindfulness—it can promptly knock out an unwholesome state of mind.

The next question is: How can we reflect in various ways to eliminate anger should we be unable to completely evict it through mindfulness? There is no shortage of ways by which one can reflect. Here we will examine a variety of them. And we believe that if you read on, by the time you reach the last page, you will be fully convinced of the undesirability and futility of anger. You would not want ever to get angry again. This conviction alone will stand you in good stead: you are already mentally predisposed towards amity, towards not getting angry, towards keeping calm and cool. With this wholesome desire and determination, you would now be less likely to give in to anger than you were previously. Furthermore, should anger arise from time to time, as it may, it would not be so strong and you will also be able to recollect and apply all the various "antidotes" that we will be discussing here.

One thing to observe is that in the application of mindfulness and wise reflection, no suppression is involved in checking the anger. Rather, the anger subsides naturally in the course of the mindfulness or reflection. In the West, it is sometimes thought that if we suppress our anger, this can be unhealthy. So, according to this school of thought, it might be a good thing to express our anger in order to release tension. On the other hand, there are also studies in the West which have shown that expressing anger overtly (i.e. openly) can also be harmful. In any case, allowing oneself to "explode" in order to release tension would not be at all compatible with the Buddhist approach. The Buddha never made such a concession, but on the contrary he asked us to return anger with love. In giving free rein to our anger, we are opening our mind to stronger defilement and creating more bad *kamma,* while at the same time we are very likely to harm or hurt another. In extreme cases, people have killed simply out of anger and victims are sometimes inno-cent members of the public.

The Buddhist techniques we are discussing here do not involve the suppression of anger. Mindfulness, as has already been pointed out, involves no suppression but is mere acknowledgement of the mental state as it occurs in us. Acknowledging and observing the anger cools it down in a natural way. And applying wise reflection also checks the anger without forceful suppression.

We should cultivate
an attitude of calmness
at all times.

Firm resolution in maintaining calmness

The art of keeping calm and tranquil is something quite lost in this modern world of ours. The hectic pace of life, impatience, the emphasis on material acquisition, indiscriminate production and consumption, the all-pervasive influence of the advertising media, and many other aspects of modern living have contributed to an erosion of moral integrity and spiritual values. They have also caused the mind to be more susceptible to restlessness, agitation, anxiety, fear and anger.

It is truly high time that we balance material progress with spiritual development, with simplicity, calmness and tranquillity. To develop this calmness, the discipline of meditation is invaluable. Taking up mindfulness meditation is one solution, but it is not within the scope of this work to explain the details of that practice. That can be gleaned from other books on the subject. The meditation of loving-kindness is another excellent practice, especially effective against all forms of anger, hatred and ill-will. It is ideal for those of an angry or hateful temperament. Thus we will explain the method of loving-kindness meditation in the latter part of this book.

Meanwhile, it is important for us to strive to cultivate and maintain an attitude of calmness and equanimity at all times. If we make a consistent and purposeful effort to do so, it is less likely that we will be carried away by turbulent emotions such as anger. Thus, from now on, we should try to maintain calmness and steadiness in all that we do. We should try to speak calmly and mindfully, not excitedly. We should apply mindfulness to check agitation and excitement whenever they arise. We should keep our bodily composure serene and calm. If we go

Consider the Buddha's
fine example.

about our daily activities calmly, mindfully and purposefully, we will come to experience a delightful peace and tranquillity. In that calm and stillness, you will find a deep reservoir of power and energy to accomplish your tasks and goals.

Thus the second "antidote" to anger is to cultivate and maintain calmness and stability. St. Abba Dorotheus put it rather well when he said: "Over whatever you have to do, even if it be very urgent and demands great care, I would not have you argue or be agitated. For rest assured, everything you do, be it great or small, is but one-eighth of the problem, whereas to keep one's state undisturbed even if thereby one should fail to accomplish the task, is the other seven-eighths. So if you are busy at some task and wish to do it perfectly, try to accomplish it — which, as I said would be one-eighth of the problem, and at the same time to preserve your state unharmed — which constitutes seven-eighths. If, however, in order to accomplish your task you would inevitably be carried away and harm yourself or another by arguing with him, you should not lose seven for the sake of preserving one-eighth."

 ## 3 Consider the Buddha's fine example

As Buddhists, we should consider the Buddha's advice and example. The Buddha often exhibited great patience in the face of extreme provocation. He never got angry but instead radiated love (*mettā*) even towards his oppressors. He did not become angry when Devadatta tried to kill him, when Cinca falsely accused him of causing

Unperturbed shall our
mind be, amidst the
angry and abusive.

her pregnancy, or when he was falsely charged with killing a female wanderer from another sect.

Not only in his last life but also in his previous lives as a *bodhisatta* (i.e. a Buddha-to-be), the Buddha showed great patience and endurance. The *Khantivādijātaka* (Birth Story of the Preacher of Forbearance) demonstrates the Bodhisatta's remarkable patience when he was an ascetic known as Khantivādi, "Preacher of Patience." In that story, the evil king Kalabu of Kasi became angry with the Bodhisatta when the latter won the admiration of the palace women with his sermons on the practice of patience. The king therefore confronted the Bodhisatta and asked: "What do you teach, recluse?" The Bodhisatta replied: "I teach forbearance, sir."

"What is this forbearance?"

"It is being without anger when people curse or strike or revile you."

The king, saying: "Now I will see the reality of your forbearance," summoned his executioner and ordered him to flog the Bodhisatta. The executioner flogged the Bodhisatta until his skin was split and the blood flowed forth. Again the king asked the Bodhisatta: "What do you teach, recluse?"

The Bodhisatta replied: "I teach forbearance, sir, but you think my forbearance is only skin-deep. My forbearance is not skin-deep, but it could not be seen by you, for my forbearance, sir, is firmly rooted within my heart."

The king next ordered the executioner to chop off the Bodhisatta's hands and feet. The executioner did so and the Bodhisatta bled profusely.

Again the king taunted the Bodhisatta: "What do you teach?"

"I teach forbearance, sir. But you think forbearance is in my hands and feet. Forbearance is not there; it is firmly rooted in a deep place within me."

The king ordered: "Cut off his ears and nose." The executioner complied. The Bodhisatta's whole body was covered with blood. When questioned again by the king, the Bodhisatta replied: "I teach forbearance, sir. But don't think that forbearance resides in my ears and nose. Forbearance is firmly rooted deep within my heart."

The king, saying, "You can sit down and extol your forbearance," kicked the Bodhisatta over the heart and walked off.

The Commander-in-Chief of the army, who was at the scene at that time, wiped the blood from the Bodhisatta's body, bandaged the ends of his hands and feet, ears and nose, and begged for forgiveness: "O ascetic, if you would be angry, be angry with the king and not with the kingdom."

The Bodhisatta replied that he bore no anger towards anyone, not even towards the king who had mutilated him. Nay, he even wished: "Long live the king; those like me do not get angry." The Bodhisatta died that day, while the king, it is said, was swallowed up by the earth for his heinous deed and was reborn in *avīci*, the Great Hell.

Such an account of the Bodhisatta's patience and self-restraint is an inspiration and a lesson to us all. If we would aspire, as Buddhists, to be true disciples of the Buddha, then we should strive to heed his admonition. In his last life, too, in the Simile of the Saw, the Buddha said that even if robbers were to cut off our limbs, we should not only refrain from anger towards them but should radiate them with loving-kindness, wishing: "May these robbers and all beings be well and happy." No doubt, it is a most difficult admonition to heed, but it does drive home the point: There is no place for anger in the Buddha's teaching. And we would do well to fill our heart with love and rout out all anger. Considering thus, we may be better poised next time to check our anger when it arises.

Consider that one day we all must die

Life's but a walking shadow, a poor player,
That struts and frets his hour upon the stage,
And then is heard no more: it is a tale
Told by an idiot, full of sound and fury,
Signifying nothing.

- Shakespeare, *Macbeth*

The others do not know that we in this world all must die.
Those who know have their quarrels calmed thereby.

- Buddha, *Dhammapada*

In the verse above, Shakespeare reminds us of our vulnerability, mortality and the foolish ways we sometimes live our lives. And the saying by the Buddha is also a timely reminder of the ever pervasive presence of death dogging our every step. Yes, isn't it true that, in the heat of the moment, we forget that we all must die one day? But when we reflect on death, we can tell ourselves: "Ah! What is the use of getting angry? Life is short. Soon we will all be dead. Getting angry or agitated will get me nowhere but just upset me all the more. Therefore, let me do

The boast of heraldry, the pomp of power,
And all that beauty, all that wealth e'er gave,
Awaits alike the inevitable hour.
The paths of glory lead but to the grave.

~Thomas Gray

what I can without becoming upset. I shall live at peace with myself and the world. After all, I seek to quarrel with nobody." Thinking in such a way, one can cool down and dispel one's anger.

In fact, it is good to reflect on death at least once a day. The Buddha taught us contemplation on death *(maraṇasati)* so that we could develop a sense of urgency in meditating and in cultivating wisdom. Reflecting on death will also stir us to make an effort to live a meaningful and fulfilling life, and not fritter our time away in unprofitable pursuits. As the *vipassanā* teacher Joseph Goldstein puts it: "If we take death as our advisor, we will live each moment with the power and fullness we would give to our last endeavour on earth."

So it is good always to remember: "Life is uncertain but death is certain." Or: "Short alas, is the life of man, limited and fleeting, full of pain and torment. One should wisely understand this, do good deeds and lead a holy life, for no mortal ever escapes death."

 ## 5 Consider the harmful effects of anger on oneself

Do you want to harm yourself? Of course, no one would want to harm himself (or herself). But whenever we are angry, we are actually harming ourselves. The meditation manual, *Visuddhimagga* (Path of Purification), states: "By being angry with another, you may or may not make him suffer, but you are certainly suffering now." And: "By getting angry you're like a man who wants to hit another and picks up a burning ember or excrement and had so first burned yourself or made

Anger is like a poison.
Would you want to
drown in it?

yourself stink. Oh, is there a person more foolish than you!" Yes, we may or may not harm the other by our anger, but we are certainly harming ourselves. How? Firstly, we are already poisoning our mind by becoming angry, for anger *(dosa)* is an unwholesome state of mind, and by being angry we are hurting and polluting our mind. As Buddhists, we should know that any unwholesome state of mind *(akusala-citta)* must lead to painful effects *(dukkha-vipāka)*. So if we do not wish to reap bad *kamma-vipāka* (kammic effects), then we would be wise to steer away from anger and all unwholesome states of mind.

As we mentioned earlier, our mental states have a bearing on our physical health. "Each thought and feeling is accompanied by a shower of brain chemicals that affects and is affected by billions of cells," says Paul Pearsall, an American doctor and researcher. Emphasizing that our health can improve with mastery over our emotions, Dr Pearsall, in his book, *Super-immunity,* wrote: "Invisible things such as thoughts and feelings can cause illness and wellness..... Germs hover constantly about us, but they do not set in and take root unless the terrain is ripe. This terrain is cultivated by our thoughts, cognitive style, feelings, and perceptions."

Another doctor, U Aung Thein, in an article on Buddhist Meditation and Bioscience, explained that unwholesome emotions can upset the biochemical balance of the body. Chemicals produced by the body as a result of these emotions can adversely affect various organs such as the thyroid, adrenal cortex, digestive tracts and reproductive organs.

Anger, for instance, causes the production of the chemical, *epinephrine,* which in turn causes a rise in the blood pressure, heart beat and oxygen consumption. Prolonged or frequent occurrence of unwholesome mental

Mirror, mirror on
the wall....

states could lead to various ailments such as peptic ulcers, indigestion, heart problems and even cancer.

Considering the dangerous effects of anger and other unwholesome mental states on both our mind and body, we should be more determined than ever not to give in to these negative emotions. We should strive to expel them promptly from our mind whenever they arise. We should be more determined to respond with equanimity and calmness in all situations.

 ### 6 Look into a mirror

An angry man or woman is a very ugly person. If, when you are angry, you were to see your contorted face in the mirror, you can be assured that you wouldn't like yourself. Perhaps all of us should carry a small mirror in our pocket so that, every time we get angry, we can quickly produce the mirror and have a good look at ourselves. That might be an instant antidote in quelling the demon in us.

Even the prettiest girl can appear ugly after some time if she habitually gets angry. Wrinkles may show before their time. She would appear to be always frowning. Or there would emerge a taint in her good looks, a sort of unpleasantness that will keep people away. On the other hand, the person who is always smiling and good-natured, who very rarely gets angry, is a truly lovely person. He or she is well-liked and welcomed wherever he or she goes.

It is said that people who are ugly now were probably hot-tempered in their previous life. The law of *kamma* dictates that a person who is of a hateful or angry temperament will, if reborn as a human being, be

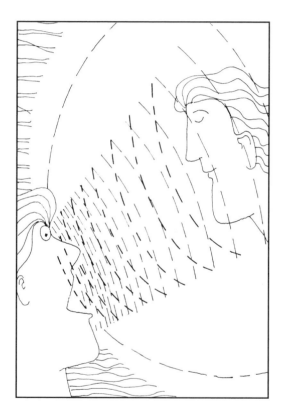

We are owners of
our deeds.

ugly or even hideous. Since we, as Buddhists, believe in the law of *kamma,* which is a natural law of cause and effect, we should refrain from getting angry. If you do get angry, think of the bad kammic effects that may befall you, and you may quickly calm down.

7 Consider that we are owners of our deeds

We are owners of our deeds. Whatever we do we will get in return. In explaining the law of *kamma,* the Buddha said: "Monks, beings are owners of their deeds. They are heirs of their deeds. Their deeds are the womb from which they spring. They are related to their deeds. Their deeds are their refuge. Whatever they do, whether good or bad, of that they will be the heir."

Considering thus, we can feel sorry for the person who is nasty or of a hateful temperament. Why? Because by being angry or nasty, he is heaping up much bad *kamma* which will bear unpleasant results one day. If he does not change his behaviour, he might even end up in hell! And if we were to respond with anger and spite, we would not be much better than him. We might even end up in hell along with him!

When we reflect on the law of *kamma* we can calm down. For the law of *kamma* is one which enjoins on us self-responsibility. Each of us is responsible for our own deeds. If a person does evil, he will have to suffer when the effect of that *kamma* ripens. On our part, we should steer clear of anger and all unwholesome attitudes.

Consider his good points.

8 Consider his good points

Everybody has some good qualities. If we consider the other person's good points, we may not get angry with him so easily. Earlier he may have helped us in some way. When we recall his good qualities and the things he may have done for us before, we will soften and cool down. Also, we should remember that nobody is perfect and that we have our faults too. The Buddha said that it is better to look at our own faults and correct them than to look at others' faults. It is better to see one fault in oneself than a thousand faults in another.

9 Freeze!

Whenever we are angry, we should not act or say anything. For in that frame of mind, what we do or say is likely to be unskilful. We might do or say something hurtful which we will later regret. Then, even though we may apologize later on, it will be too late, for the harm has already been done. The person who was hurt might not be able to help changing his attitude or feelings towards us.

Thus, whenever anger arises, we should freeze and be like a block of wood. Only after we have quelled the anger should we say or do anything. So we fall back on the principle of acting only from a cool and calm mind. In that way, what we do will be done well, and there will be no cause for remorse or regret later.

Whenever anger arises,
we should freeze and
be like a block of wood.

Nobody is free from blame

The Buddha once told a disciple, Atula, "This is a thing of old, Atula, not only of today; they blame him who remains silent, they blame him who talks much, they blame him who speaks in moderation; none in the world is left unblamed." If we observe for ourselves, we can see that this is quite true: Nobody in this world is completely free from blame. No matter what we do, someone somewhere might still find fault with us. Understanding the nature of existence thus, we should not get upset or angry when we are blamed.

What we can do, however, is to examine the grounds for the blame. If it is true that we are wrong, then we can calmly take steps to rectify the mistake. But if we have been unjustly blamed, we need not be perturbed. We can explain the reasons behind our action and why the blame is unjustified. After doing all that we can, we should not be concerned about undue blame. We should exercise equanimity and reflect on the fact that even the Buddha was not spared from blame. For example, during his time, the Buddha was criticized for eating meat, falsely accused of having an affair with Cinca, and charged with murdering a woman wanderer.

What is important is to do the right thing, or to do the best that we can under the circumstances. When we have done thus, we will be blameless, and no wise person, no one who understands our position and the reasons behind our action, will ever blame us. Only those who are foolish, or those who may not understand the reasons and conditions behind our action, might blame us. That should be accepted as something unavoidable in life; for no matter what we do, we might still

None in the world is
free from blame.

be blamed or criticized. All that lies within our power is to do what we must skilfully enough to minimize the incidence of blame. After that, if we are still blamed, there is little we can do or need do about it.

 ## Why are we angry?

If we look into the question of why we get angry, we will realize that it is because we still have an ego, perhaps a big one at that. We still identify with an *attā*, an "I", an ego. That is why we feel slighted and get angry. If we do not identify with an "I", and have understood well the Buddha's teaching of *anattā* (non-self), we wouldn't get upset or angry no matter how much we are provoked. During his time, the Buddha was provoked and challenged on many occasions, yet he never got angry. Not once in the scriptures do we find an occasion when the Buddha became angry. On the contrary, the scriptures emphasize that the Buddha is one who has rooted out all anger, one who is incapable of getting angry. Thus, even when the Buddha should have occasion to firmly reproach an errant monk or a disciple, he would do it calmly, without anger.

Similarly, the *arahants* who have attained enlightenment are also incapable of getting angry. The Buddha's chief disciple, Sāriputta, for example, was renowned for his great patience and humility. Once a group of people was praising Sāriputta's qualities, saying: "Such great patience has our noble Elder that even when people abuse and strike him, he feels no trace of anger." A disbelieving brahmin retorted: "Who is this that never gets angry?" and set out to provoke the Elder. One day he approached Sāriputta from behind and gave him a hard blow on

Why are we angry?

the back. Venerable Sāriputta, remarking, "What was that?" continued on his alms round without even looking back. The brahmin at once felt remorse and, falling at the feet of the Elder, asked for forgiveness. "For what?" asked Sāriputta, mildly. "To test your patience, I struck you," the penitent brahmin replied. "Very well, I pardon you."

The brahmin then invited Sāriputta to have lunch at his house. But those who saw the assault were enraged and wanted to beat up the brahmin. Sāriputta stopped them by asking: "Was it you, or me, he struck?" "It was you, reverend sir." "Well, if it was me he struck, he has begged my pardon. Go your way." And in that way the magnanimous Sāriputta dismissed the mob.

Sāriputta's humility was as great as his patience. On another occasion, the Elder was reproached by a seven-year-old novice for not wearing his robe properly. It seems that, through momentary negligence, the Elder had left a corner of his lower robe hanging down. When this was pointed out to him, Sāriputta, instead of becoming annoyed for being reproached by a mere seven-year-old novice, at once stepped aside and rearranged his robe properly. Then he stood before the novice with folded hands, saying: "Now it is correct, teacher."

Such accounts of the conduct of an *arahant* are an inspiration and a lesson to us. Why are the *arahants* incapable of getting angry? Because they have rooted out all attachment to the concept of a self or ego. Having no self or ego concept, they do not feel, "It is I who was slighted." Or: "How dare this mere novice of seven correct me, Sāriputta, the chief disciple of the Buddha." Such thoughts never occurred to Sāriputta because he, having penetrated well the *anattā* (non-self) teaching of the Buddha, had rooted out all anger and pride.

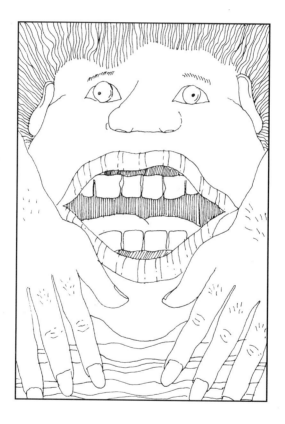

Now, what is it you are angry with?
Is it the head hair? body hair?
nails? teeth? skin? ....

So the next time we get angry, we should understand that it is because we still identify with an "I" or ego. If we can then contemplate on the truth of *anattā,* that there is ultimately no "I" here, that "I" is merely a conventional term and concept, we might be able to cool down and dispel incipient anger. Furthermore, we can consider how Sāriputta, despite his position as the Buddha's chief disciple, never lost his temper even when rudely insulted and provoked. Reflecting thus, we might be able to restrain our anger.

 ## 12 Who is angry?

The next question to consider is, "Who is angry?" "What is getting angry?" *Attā?* I? Remember, in the ultimate sense, neither you nor the person you are angry with exists. After all, what are we but only mind and matter, elements and processes.

Thus, in the *Visuddhimagga,* we are taught to reflect by dissecting the body into parts: "Now, what is it you are angry with? Is it the head hair you are angry with? Or body hair? Or nails? ... Or is it urine you are angry with? Or alternatively, is it the earth element in the head hair you are angry with? Or the water element? Or the fire element? Or is it the air element you are angry with? ... Is it the material aggregate *(khandha)* that you are angry with, or the feeling aggregate, the perception aggregate, the formations aggregate, the consciousness aggregate you are angry with? Or is it the eye base? ..." When we reflect in this way, our anger will find no foothold and will subside.

Or we can consider that we are all made of mind and matter. And this mind and matter is constantly changing. The mind especially

Hi! Don't you know
we are all one
big family?

changes very fast, one consciousness arising and passing away very quickly. It is said that in a flash of a lightning, or in a wink of an eye, millions of thought-moments arise and pass away. So what are you angry with? With whom are you angry? The mind and matter *(nāma-rūpa)* that you are angry with has already passed. Many sets of mind and matter have since taken their place. By reflecting in this way too, we can make our anger subside.

13 Consider that we are all related

Beginningless, says the Buddha, is the round of rebirths. We have been traversing *saṁsāra,* this wandering and faring on, for so long that at one time or another we have all been related to each other in one way or another. Hence the Buddha said: "Bhikkhus, it is not easy to find a being who has not formerly been your mother ... your father ... your brother ... your sister ... your son ... your daughter." So it would be unbecoming of us to harbour any hate against the person who had been related to us in our past lives. Thinking in this way too, we can make our anger subside.

14 Forgiveness

One of the reasons for our anger is our inability to forgive and forget. So we flare up easily, and in the aftermath we tend to nurse bitterness, resentment or animosity for some grievance (real or

C'mon, cheer up!
Forgive
everyone...

even ourselves!

imagined) done us. Although we may think that we have forgiven, deep down in our heart we may not have totally forgiven. Consciously or unconsciously, we may still be harbouring some bitterness or resentment. If we can learn to let go, to forgive spontaneously and completely, we would live more lightly and happily—without having to carry around the weight of our resentment and anger.

Forgiveness has been rightly called "the most tender part of love," and "the fragrance the violet sheds on the heel that has crushed it." "It ought to be like a cancelled note, torn in two and burned up, so that it can never be shown against the man." If we truly love, if we have strong loving-kindness *(mettā)*, we should be able to forgive fully, wholeheartedly, without any condition or reservations.

What do we forgive? We forgive whatever wrongs others might have done us, just as we would like others to forgive us for the wrongs we have done them. We seek no revenge. We refrain from getting angry, from saying or doing things to hurt or spite the one who may have wronged us. We forgive, harbouring no grudges or ill-will, understanding that all of us still have our faults and weaknesses.

Just as we forgive others, we should forgive ourselves too, for sometimes we might have done something wrong in the past and we now find it difficult to forgive ourselves. We suffer from regret and remorse. Such remorse, which causes us mental upset and agony, is also unwholesome. The Buddha stated that we should not mope over some wrong we have done, but should resolve not to repeat our mistake, and where possible make amends. We should put the unhappy episode behind us, and not brood over it with pangs of remorse. If recollection should arise, we should note it (i.e. exercise mindfulness) and not agonize over the matter. We should firmly put aside the thought, understanding that there is nothing more we can do apart from making amends and being determined not to repeat the error. Sometimes we impose great demands and expectations on ourselves. But we should accept our human failings too and that we all cannot become saints overnight. We can't push it, but if we work at it consistently, patiently, we will eventually reach our goal. What we need is patience, determination and perseverance.

15 Review the benefits of loving-kindness

When we consider the benefits of cultivating loving-kindness, we will be disinclined to get angry. The Buddha has stated that the practitioner of loving-kindness meditation can expect eleven benefits: He or she sleeps easily; wakes up fresh; dreams no bad dreams; is dear to human beings; is dear to non-human beings; *devas* (deities) protect him; fire, poison and weapons do not harm him; he gains concentration easily; his features are serene; he dies unconfused, peacefully as if falling asleep; if he has not attained arahatship he will be reborn after death in the sublime *Brahma-*realm. More discussion on these benefits will be taken up in the section on the practice of loving-kindness *(mettā)* meditation. But even when put in a nutshell, these benefits are highly desirable and should be "tempting" enough for us to quell our anger and keep cool. On the other hand, if we give in to anger we might lose these advantages. Contemplating thus would also act as a deterrent to us from succumbing to anger.

16 Give a gift

In some cases, we can give a gift. For example, there may be a person who seems to dislike us and who often says bad things about us. It would be easy in such cases to respond with anger and frustration, and to hit back. But that is not the way for a disciple of the Buddha, whose motto is never to return hate with hate but to respond with love instead. So we can rise up to the challenge and do a most difficult thing by buying the person a gift! It would be a sign of our magnanimity and big-heartedness, that despite the bad intent of the other, we harbour no ill-will. We could then be cool and steady, knowing that we have refused to be drawn into any conflict or to seethe with anger or ill-will. And the other party too might well be touched by our noble gesture. He might soften in his stance against us. He might even become friendly. So giving a gift may do wonders.

Conclusion

We have come to the end of this section. In the foregoing, we have discussed a number of attitudes we can adopt in curbing anger and keeping calm. We hope that the reader, having read this far, will make an even stronger resolution to give up anger and cultivate love. In the next section, we shall discuss the practice of *mettā-bhāvanā* — loving-kindness meditation.

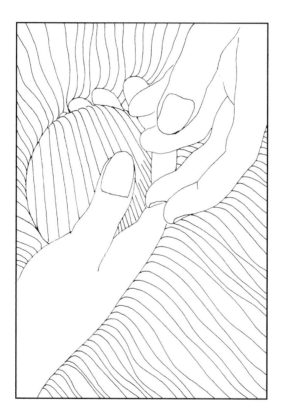

A gift to melt the heart!

Summary of Antidotes

1   First rule: Mindfulness.

2   Firm resolution in maintaining calmness.

3   Consider the Buddha's fine example.

4   Consider that one day we all must die.

5   Consider the harmful effects of anger on oneself.

6   Look into a mirror.

7   Consider that we are owners of our deeds.

8   Consider his good points.

9   Freeze!

10   Nobody is free from blame.

11   Why are we angry?

12   Who is angry?

13   Consider that we are all related.

14   Forgiveness.

15   Review the benefits of loving-kindness.

16   Give a gift.

[Love is] the joy of the good,
the wonder of the wise,
the amazement of the gods.

- Plato

LOVE

hat is love? What is its quality? How many kinds of love are there? Is love as taught by the Buddha different from our general understanding of love? What in the first place is our understanding of love? These are questions we can ask even before we start to talk or write about love.

Love is a very much used and popular word, part and parcel of our daily vocabulary. We write about it, speak about it, read about it. Many of us consider it the very essence of life. We have sayings like "Love is a many splendoured thing," "Love means never having to say sorry," "Love makes the world go round." We throw about slogans such as "Make love, not war."

Yet can we really answer the question: "What is love?" The dictionary defines love variantly as a warm, kind feeling; a deep and tender feeling of affection for, or attachment or devotion to, a person or persons; a feeling of brotherhood and goodwill toward all people; a strong, usually passionate affection of one person for another, based in part on

sexual attraction; and sexual intercourse. Too often, when we think and talk about love, we fuse these different senses of the word into one vague, ambiguous cloud.

It is apt to start by defining the kind of love we are going to discuss here. It is that warm, kind feeling for others, wishing for their welfare; it is soft, caring and tender; it is unselfish, not expecting anything in return; it is lofty, transcending all barriers of creed, sex, race and nationality. It extends to all living beings in the universe, including insects, fish, animals and spirits.

This love is not petty or passionate attachment to a person; it has no sexual connotation; it is not sensual or sexual gratification. True, we acknowledge that there is love between lovers, and between husbands and wives. There may be care and tenderness in their relationship. But their love is not unconditional. It is mixed with a strong sensual or sexual attraction. It is liable to change if one party does not reciprocate or cannot satisfy the needs or desires of the other. So since such love is conditional, limiting and subjective, it is radically different from the lofty, totally selfless and transcendental kind of love we are discussing here.

While on the subject of love, it is pertinent too to discuss the question of lust. What is lust? Again the dictionary defines it as a desire to gratify the senses, bodily appetite; sexual desire; excessive sexual desire especially as seeking unrestrained gratification; overmastering desire. Thus we can see that in the love between two partners a certain degree of lust is involved. Sexual desire itself involves a desire to gratify the senses, and that, as we know, can be very strong and overpowering, blinding, passionate, even obsessive. It can give rise to strong fits of jealousy, anger and depression when the loved one has eyes for another, or when the love is not reciprocated.

So again this is not the kind of love we are discussing here, as it is conditional and subordinate to wants and desires. Nevertheless, there are undeniable feelings of tenderness, care and affection between lovers and between husbands and wives, even though these feelings may be conditional and based on sexual attraction. Perhaps, starting from a less lofty kind of love, lovers and husbands and wives too can work at expanding their understanding of love. Perhaps then they can eventually appreciate and develop that loftier kind of love that transcends all barriers, limitations and conditions.

So the kind of love we are concerned with is the love that seeks and delights in the welfare of others. It is lofty and selfless, expecting nothing in return, not even appreciation or gratitude. It gives just for the sake of giving. It finds delight in seeing joy and happiness light up in another's eyes or face. That is sufficient reward, making all the effort and "labour of love" worthwhile. Such love wishes for others only what is good, that they be happy and be far from all pain and suffering.

Thus, in the traditional Buddhist "love formula," we wish: "May all beings be well and happy! May they be free from harm and danger! May they be free from mental suffering! May they be free from physical suffering! May they take care of themselves happily!"

The Buddha's life itself is an exemplification of love and compassion. It was because of his *mettā* (love) and *karuṇā* (compassion) that he renounced the luxurious worldly life he was living to seek the way to the ending of all suffering. Having found it, he then shared it with all beings, wanting them to experience the happiness of liberation, the happiness of *Nibbāna*, that can be attained in this very life through the purification of the mind. And the Buddha exhorted his disciples to go far and wide to spread his teachings to as many people as possible so that they too might taste the nectar of liberation. The Great Teacher himself set the lead by travelling throughout India teaching tirelessly to all strata of society for forty-five years after his Enlightenment until his death at the ripe age of eighty.

The Buddha urged his monks and disciples to radiate loving-kindness frequently. He asked them to suffuse all quarters of the world with a mind of love that is "far-reaching, widespread and immeasurable." In whatever posture they may be, whether walking, standing, sitting or lying down, he urged them to radiate thoughts of love to all beings. In the teachings of the Buddha, there is no room for even an iota of enmity or ill-will. Such love is the highest and noblest. It is not easy to love fully, wholeheartedly, without expecting anything in return. Certainly, it would be extremely difficult for us to develop this love to the degree of purity achieved by the Buddha—a love that envelopes all beings, that is not burning or searing but is cooling and even, having been tempered by wisdom and equanimity.

We begin to cultivate such a kind of love when we practise loving-kindness and *vipassanā* insight meditation. *Mettā* or loving-kindness meditation is a particularly effective weapon against hatred and anger. And through the practice of *vipassanā* meditation, love and compassion will also blossom when we realize that all of us are fellow-sufferers in *saṁsāra*. In the following pages, we will confine our discussion to the development of *mettā*. The practice of *vipassanā* had been covered by us in another booklet entitled *Invitation to Vipassanā*.

He abides pervading one quarter with a mind imbued with loving-kindness, likewise the second, likewise the third, likewise the fourth; so above, below, around and everywhere, and to all as to himself, he abides pervading the all-encompassing world with a mind imbued with loving-kindness, abundant, exalted, immeasurable, without hostility and without ill will.

- The Buddha

METTĀ BHĀVANĀ
THE CULTIVATION OF LOVING-KINDNESS

 ettā or loving-kindness meditation is particularly suitable for one who has an angry temperament, i.e. a person who gets angry easily, who nurses grudges and finds difficulty in forgetting and forgiving, who harbours animosity and hatred. Hot-tempered persons and those troubled by anger have found, happily, that their temper has gone after regular practice. And even for those who are not ill-tempered, much benefit can be gained from this practice, for all of us do get annoyed or irritated from time to time and the practice then helps us to keep more cool. Though one may talk about benefits now, the practice of *mettā* is ultimately self-fulfilling. By constant practice of *mettā*, one will eventually develop the kind of love that loves just for the sake of loving, for relieving the suffering of others and promoting goodwill, good cheer and happiness. The benefits we speak about here then become secondary or insignificant. But in the beginning they can be looked upon as incentives for taking up the practice.

The mind becomes dead-still
like a candle flame that would,
in the absence of any breeze,
glow steadily without even a flicker.

One of the objectives of meditation is to gain concentration or one-pointedness of mind. When the mind is fixed on one object, it settles and becomes calm and tranquil. At that time the tendency of the mind to wander has been stopped, at least while the mind is fixed or absorbed in its object of meditation. It is a very cooling and soothing experience when we reach this kind of calmness, the calmness of no-thought, the calmness of a one-pointed mind focused undistractedly on its object. The mind becomes dead-still like a candle flame that, in the absence of any breeze, glows steadily without even a flicker.

The principle then is to make the mind one-pointed, fixed on its object of meditation. In the case of loving-kindness meditation, the object is the concept of love, the wishing of well-being for all beings. There are various formulas one can use in radiating *mettā* and obtaining this one-pointedness of mind. Here we will discuss one of the methods that can be successfully practised.

First the formula is expressed in four lines:
May all beings be free from harm and danger.
May they be free from mental suffering.
May they be free from physical suffering.
May they take care of themselves happily.

These four lines can be easily memorized. The meditator needs to recite these lines over and over again in his mind. Only mental recitation is required, not verbal recitation. If the mind is likened to a computer, the idea is to programme it with thoughts of wishing well for others until it overflows with these thoughts, overflows with love. As one recites mentally the mind will start to concentrate on its object of love, wishing well for others. Extraneous thoughts are kept away and eventually can gain no entry at all. At that time the mind becomes concentrated, one-pointed, and one experiences that special stillness and tranquillity.

Before we go further we need to explain the meaning of the four lines we are to recite. Once their import is understood, we will naturally know what is meant or implied as we radiate thoughts of love.

 ## May all beings be free from harm and danger:

There are two kinds of harm and danger—internal and external. *Internal* refers to our defilements *(kilesa)*, such as greed, hatred, delusion, worry, anxiety, etc., which cause us mental suffering. *External* refers to dangers such as accidents, natural calamities (fire, floods, landslides, earthquakes, etc.), and danger from people who might want to harm us. Nobody wants these dangers whether internal or external though the internal dangers, i.e. the defilements, are even worse than the external ones. We are our own greatest enemies. If we can overcome the internal defilements, we can face external obstacles without fear or anxiety.

 ## May they be free from mental suffering:

Mental suffering ranges from the subtle to the gross. It includes such states as worry, anxiety, fear, depression, sorrow, despair or any unwholesome state of mind that can bring about mental turmoil, distress or agony. Nobody wants mental suffering of any kind. We want to be calm, peaceful and happy always.

May they be free from physical suffering:

Physical suffering extends from minor bodily discomforts, aches and illnesses, such as colds and headaches, to serious ailments such as cancer and heart disease. Nobody wants to suffer any kind of physical discomfort.

May they take care of themselves happily:

Here we wish that beings live from day to day smoothly and happily. All of us need to go about discharging our various chores and responsibilities. Students need to study while adults have to earn a living. We need to get along with the people we come into contact with, such as our colleagues, friends, relatives, family members and loved ones. Unless we relate well with others, life can be difficult. So we want to be on good terms with everybody, free from conflicts, with lots of goodwill and sympathetic understanding. Then we also need to be able to discharge our duties well. We need to do our work efficiently, otherwise we will have a lot of problems.

Furthermore we need to take care of this body and mind daily. As for the body, we need to feed it, clothe it, give it medicine when

May all beings be free from harm and danger.
May they be free from mental suffering.
May they be free from physical suffering.
May they take care of themselves happily.

necessary, answer the calls of nature, etc. These too are our daily chores and we need to go about them smoothly, cheerfully. We also must take care of the mind. We need to clean it too by doing meditation, exercising restraint, cultivating the right attitudes and reflecting wisely.

So when we say *"May they (all beings) take care of themselves happily,"* it is a comprehensive statement covering all these various aspects of daily living. Thus one can appreciate that the four lines, beginning *"May all beings be free from harm and danger,"* are all-comprehensive, covering what everybody would or could wish for. When we understand the full import of the four lines, the radiation of our *mettā* will be more meaningful.

PRACTICE PROPER

One sits in the usual meditation posture, cross-legged on the floor with the back straight (or on a chair for those who are unable to sit on the floor). One closes the eyes, keeps the body relaxed and recites the four lines mentally (i.e. not aloud or verbally but only mentally).

One recites the four lines again and again for ten minutes, thirty minutes, up to an hour. One recites continuously a hundred times, a thousand times, a hundred thousand times, a million times. It does not matter how long or how many times one recites. One just keeps on reciting and reciting and reciting. It is a method of programming the mind—programming the mind with thoughts of loving-kindness and goodwill for all beings. As we recite we need not ponder the meaning of the words as we already know their import. Gradually and naturally, as we recite, the feeling of loving-kindness and goodwill for all beings will awaken in us. We will be filled with a feeling of harmlessness; we will not want to harm or hurt anybody, or to harbour any anger or ill-will against anybody.

As we keep on reciting and radiating *mettā* in this way, the mind will become one-pointed and settle down on its own accord. It will grow calm, tranquil and peaceful. The words may flow smoothly by themselves like a tape-recorder that has been turned on. Sometimes as the mind settles down we may forget to recite. Or we may jumble up the lines. This is all right. Once we are aware, we just have to recite again as usual. In this way the concentration will develop naturally. One need not yearn for or anticipate good concentration; it will come on its own accord as one does the work of mental recitation.

HOW CONCENTRATION COMES ABOUT

As we mentally recite the lines we are radiating *mettā*. As the recitation flows the mind becomes focused or concentrated on one object—i.e. loving-kindness, or the radiation of that loving-kindness. At that time the mind stops wandering and flows along with the *mettā* radiation. When wandering stops, when thinking, worrying, reflecting, planning, etc., stops, the mind attains concentration, one-pointedness. In that concentration, tranquillity and peace of mind will arise naturally. One will feel happy, light and comfortable. It is a very pleasant and welcome experience—a great relief from the mind's wearisome preoccupation with its restless round of thoughts, worries and reflections. This calmness of concentration is very soothing. It is a superior, non-sensual kind of happiness which "spiritual" persons indulge in. This is the kind of happiness which the Buddha praises—not the sensual, worldly happiness derived from pleasant sights, pleasant sounds, tastes, touch, etc. Sensual happiness is described by the Buddha as low and vulgar, bringing suffering as it defiles the mind. The happiness or pleasure of concentration, however, has to be experienced to be appreciated. Once the meditator has a taste of it, his attraction to sense pleasures will loosen; he will no longer be a slave to the sensual lure. Having tasted the superior spiritual happiness, he will be better able to check his sensual desires, preferring the superior spiritual happiness of meditation.

Technically, when the mind is concentrated, five hindrances *(nīvarana)* are overcome: (1) sensual desire; (2) aversion, ill-will or anger; (3) sloth and torpor, i.e. drowsiness, sleepiness, lethargy; (4) restlessness and distraction, worry and anxiety; and (5) doubt (about the practice, about one's ability to concentrate, etc.). Thus when one gains concentration the mind becomes steady and the five hindrances, which are unwholesome mental states, will naturally fall away. When the hindrances fall away, the mind becomes still more deeply concentrated. It does not crave for sensual pleasures; it does not boil with anger or ill-will; it is not sleepy or sluggish; restless or worried; or doubtful. Consequently it grows calm, content and peaceful. In this calmness the five *jhanic* (absorption) factors become prominent. They are:

1. *Vitakka,* which is usually translated as initial application of mind. This means that the mind is hitting the target, is being well-directed to the object of meditation; it does not wander off elsewhere.

2. *Vicāra,* or sustained application of mind. This means the mind sticks with the object, stays with it, rubs into the object, impinges on it.

Vitakka directs the mind to the object while *vicāra* causes it to impinge on the object and stay there.

3. As a consequence, *pīti*, rapture, arises. The yogi feels joyful and light. He enjoys pleasant sensations, vibrant waves of delight, moving through his body. Sometimes he may experience uplifting *pīti*, i.e. his hands and legs may suddenly rise, lift or jerk up, or his body may even float up, or he may feel as if he is floating in the air.

4. *Sukha*, happiness, also develops. This *sukha* is akin to *pīti* except that it is more refined. So when *sukha* is prominent, the gross kind of *pīti* will subside and the yogi feels very light and at ease. As stated in the scriptures it is a "comfortable abiding here and now." The yogi is content and comfortable. In this state he does not yearn for sensual pleasures, which appear coarse, burning and agitating, rather than calming and soothing like the happiness of wholesome concentration.

5. *Ekaggatā*, one-pointedness of mind, becomes prominent. The mind grows steady and still, becomes one-pointed like an unflickering lamp-flame in a windless place, or like a firmly fixed pillar that cannot be shaken. The yogi who experiences this *ekaggatā* can distinctly feel his mind become unwavering, like an unshakeable post or rock.

These five jhanic factors are also present in access concentration (*upacāra-samādhi*), the concentration that occurs in the neighbourhood of *jhāna*, the concentration that heralds the arrival of *jhāna*. But in the access state they are still not firm and the hindrances can still intrude and disrupt the concentration. However, when the mind attains *jhāna* the factors become firm and the hindrances are kept at a distance. Thus there is less likelihood of the *jhāna* being interrupted and the yogi can now meditate for five, ten, twenty, thirty minutes, an hour or more at a stretch without any disruption by the hindrances. How long he can stay in this state will depend on his skill in practice and the strength of his concentration *(samādhi)*. Even when interruption occurs he should be able to easily regain his concentration by continuing to radiate *mettā*. It is stated in the Commentaries that should a skilled meditator lose his *jhāna* for some trivial reason, he can reinstate it without difficulty.

Mettā-bhāvanā is one of the four *brahma-vihāras* (divine abidings) — meditations which consist of *mettā* (love), *karuṇā* (compassion), *muditā* (altruistic joy) and *upekkhā* (equanimity). According to the *Visuddhi-magga*, one can attain up to three *jhānas* in *mettā, karuṇā* and *muditā* while the fourth *jhāna* can be reached in *upekkhā*. For the cultivation of *jhāna*, exercises are prescribed in the *Visuddhimagga*, but space does not permit us to elaborate on them here. Nevertheless, a yogi who radiates according to the four-line formula we have discussed can attain a good level of concentration. If he practises diligently and consistently, he might even attain a jhanic state of consciousness, or his practice might serve as a foundation for later development of *jhāna*. For as we have discussed earlier, the principle in developing concentration is that the five hindrances must be kept at bay and the five jhanic factors must become strong and prominent.

HOW LONG SHOULD ONE RADIATE?

One should radiate *mettā* for as long as possible. In intensive practice one radiates day and night, all the time, alternating sitting with walking, and during daily activities such as eating, bathing, washing, etc. One could practise for days, weeks and months intensively in this manner.

But people who are unable to practise intensively should practise as much as they can. After getting up in the morning you can radiate from ten minutes to an hour. Even a five-minute radiation of *mettā* is still better than no radiation at all. In the course of the day, as you go about your daily chores, you can radiate anytime, anywhere. You can radiate while you are walking here and there, while you are in the office, in the work-place, while eating, bathing, etc. Radiating by reciting mentally according to the four lines is simple and will eventually come very easily and smoothly. After work too, in the evening or at night, you can radiate while sitting in the meditation posture. When going to bed you can also radiate until you fall asleep.

As one practises consistently one will feel radiantly happy and eventually one cannot help but be full of goodwill for all people. One will harbour no hate or enmity, nor will one have any desire to become involved in conflicts and quarrels. One also will not get angry or irritated easily. One will become more patient and tolerant. It is a great and effective practice. All of us should make it a habit to radiate *mettā*. The Buddha himself radiated *mettā* daily and exhorted his disciples to do the same.

Radiating *mettā* is a good way to keep the mind wholesome. Too often our mind wanders at random, reacting to all stimuli with greed, anger, delusion, worry, anxiety, etc. But when we radiate *mettā* we substitute wholesome thoughts for unwholesome thoughts. Consequently our mind collects itself and becomes easily concentrated in whatever we do. Distractions are curbed and this leads to less worry and more efficiency in our daily tasks.

RADIATING TO ONESELF

Initially, when you begin to practise *mettā* you can radiate briefly to yourself:

May I be free from harm and danger.

May I be free from mental suffering.

May I be free from physical suffering.

May I take care of myself happily.

However, you need not radiate long in this manner as this phase is only a preparation for the main practice. Perhaps you can repeat the lines about ten times or for just a few minutes when you begin sitting. After that you can switch over to radiating *mettā* to others, thinking that just as you wish these good things for yourself, you would wish the same for all beings. Subsequently you can stop radiating to yourself altogether and begin at once by radiating *mettā* to others. It is already understood that when you radiate to others, you would also wish the same for yourself.

The *Visuddhimagga* says that one can never gain absorption (*jhāna*) by radiating to oneself. So radiating to oneself serves the sole purpose of making oneself an example, by thinking that just as one wishes well for oneself one wishes the same for others. It is to help arouse the good-will and desire for the welfare and happiness of others.

ALTERNATIVE MODES OF RADIATION

In addition to radiating collectively to all beings, one can also radiate specifically to a certain person or a group of persons. One can radiate to a friend, a colleague, a superior, a teacher, a spouse, a loved one, relatives, parents, children, etc. Wherever one may be one can radiate, contemplating: *May all the beings who are around me here be free from harm and danger....* One can radiate to specific groups such as to all females (i.e. all females including the animals, insects and spirits), all males, all *ariyas* (i.e. Noble Ones who have attained sainthood), all *anariyas* (i.e. ordinary beings who have not attained sainthood), all humans, all *devas* (deities) and all *apāya* beings (i.e. those suffering in the four woeful states of hell, the animal world, ghost and *asura* [demon] worlds).

One can radiate in all directions—that is, to all beings in the north, south, east, west, northeast, northwest, southeast, southwest, below and above. One can also radiate according to locality: first to all beings in the home, then extending out to the neighbourhood, district, town, country, the world and the universe.

Thus, as we see, we can exercise a lot of versatility in doing *mettā*. It is really an interesting practice. In the *Visuddhimagga*, the practice for the cultivation of *jhāna* begins with the radiation to an individual: first a loved one, then a dearly loved one, followed by a neutral person and an enemy (i.e. a person who is hostile to us). In that procedure, since one is just beginning and starting with a specific individual as an object, it will surely not be advisable to radiate to a member of the opposite sex, as there is the danger of sensual desire or lust arising and "contaminating" the purity of one's *mettā*. But when one is radiating towards all beings, the scope of one's meditation is universal and obviously includes both males and females. For the initial cultivation of *jhāna*, when one selects a specific individual, one should not pick a member of the opposite sex. But eventually when one has become conversant with the practice there is no reason why one cannot—for the purpose of radiating *mettā* and not for the cultivation of *jhāna*—radiate to a member of the opposite sex. For *mettā* is love, and it would not make sense if we cannot even radiate this love to our mother or father, grandparent, or to our spouse and children just because they are of the opposite sex. So we may understand that the practice prescribed in the *Visuddhimagga* is only with regard to the cultivation of jhanic concentration when it would be prudent not to pick an individual of the opposite sex. Later on, however, one should be able to radiate to anybody, for *mettā* would not be *mettā* if it is not all-encompassing and all-embracing, transcending all barriers with regard to race, creed, sex, etc. But whenever one radiates to one of the opposite sex on an individual basis, one should always guard against the intrusion of lust or sensual desire.

The *Visuddhimagga* also states that one should not radiate to a dead person as one will not be able to gain concentration by doing so. When a person is dead, he has passed on to a new rebirth and it would seem that a deceased person would not be a suitable subject for the cultivation of *jhāna* in *mettā* meditation. If, however, we are not practising for the purpose of attaining *jhāna* or deep concentration, but simply for the sake of radiating *mettā*, we can contemplate in this manner: *May so and so, in whatever rebirth he has now taken, be free from harm and danger* ... In my opinion it would be harmless to do so as the mind that wishes well for others will always be wholesome.

PRACTISING
MINDFULNESS
AND METTĀ

 he unified practice of *mettā* and mindfulness can be a powerful combination. For example, in daily life instead of letting our mind flit here and there we can try to be mindful of our daily activities and mental states. Then from time to time we can alternate this mindfulness with radiation of *mettā*. In that way, our mind will be kept wholesome most of the time—with *mettā* or mindfulness practice. We will gain better concentration in our daily tasks. We will worry less and live more lightly and cheerfully.

As for formal sitting meditation, a yogi should find a balance between *mettā* and *vipassanā* (insight or mindfulness) meditation practice. *Vipassanā* gives us wisdom and understanding of impermanence while *mettā* is a *samatha* subject and can thus only bring about tranquillity. So one should never neglect *vipassanā*. Initially while one is learning *mettā*, one may, of course, need to spend more time on practising it intensively. But after one has gained some skill and progress in the practice, one should balance it with *vipassanā*. It is for the yogi to find his or her own balance. For example, one could do a few minutes of *mettā* and then switch to *vipassanā*. Or if one has done a sitting of *mettā* in the morning, one could do *vipassanā* in the evening. Ultimately, it is for the yogi to find a balance suitable for his or her own temperament.

Love is swift, sincere, pious,

pleasant, generous, strong, patient,

faithful, prudent, long-suffering, manly, and

never seeking her own; for

wheresoever a man seeketh his own,

there he falleth from love.

- Thomas a` Kempis

BENEFITS
OF **METTĀ**

 person who practises *mettā* consistently can expect eleven benefits.

 He sleeps easily: *Mettā* meditation is a good cure for insomnia. One need not resort to sleeping pills and tranquillizers, which may have dangerous side-effects. So those with insomnia should take up *mettā* practice. One can even radiate until one falls asleep. In the *Visuddhimagga*, it is stated that the *mettā*-meditator

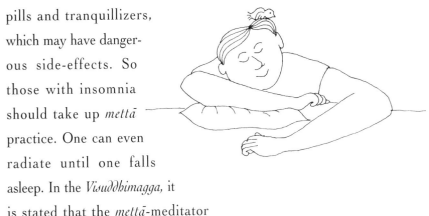

falls asleep as if entering upon a meditative attainment. Furthermore, he sleeps comfortably; he does not toss and turn, nor does he snore as other people may do in their sleep.

He wakes up fresh like a flower open-ing: Instead of groaning or yawning or turning over as others do, he wakes comfortably without contortions. He is ready to take on a new day—with optimism and cheerfulness.

He has no bad dreams: He does not dream of himself being chased by bandits, wanting to run and being unable to run, falling over a cliff or into a hole, or being haunted by ghosts, etc. Instead, if he dreams, he dreams pleasant or auspicious dreams, such as of flying through the air, seeing beautiful sights, or listening to the Dhamma and making offerings, etc. Or he might sleep soundly without any dreams.

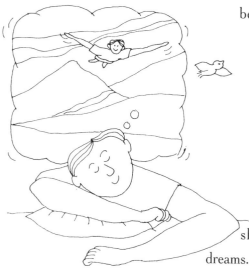

He is dear to human beings: This means he will have no enemies. People like him because of his *mettā*-nature or habit of radiating love. He will make friends easily and get along well with others. People may feel his positive mental energy, the vibrations of loving-kindness which he is always radiating.

These are valuable benefits, for having no enemies means not having to worry about people wanting to harm us. Having friends also makes life happier. Furthermore, we will find people helpful and co-operative wherever we go.

 He is dear to non-human beings: Non-human beings such as spirits and animals will also relate well towards him. And that is nice too. We needn't worry about ghosts haunting us or harming us, or dogs barking and snapping at us, or snakes biting us.

Here it is apt to relate an incident that occurred during the Buddha's time. Once, a group of monks meditating in the forest were disturbed by some spirits. The spirits took fearsome forms and made dreadful noises to frighten the monks. The monks then fled to the Buddha, who advised them to go back to the forest and radiate *mettā*. The monks did so and the spirits not only stopped haunting them but also protected them. The Commentaries state that the spirits even swept the monks' resting places and prepared warm water for them. By the end of their three-month stay in the forest all the monks attained arahatship.

In another account mentioned in the *Visuddhimagga*, a monk named Visakha was preparing to depart from a forest monastery in the Island of Tambapanni (Sri Lanka) when a tree spirit appeared to him, crying.

He is dear to all beings.

The monk asked: "What are you weeping for?" The spirit replied: "Because you are going away." The monk asked: "What good does my living here do you?"

"Venerable sir, as long as you live here, non-human beings treat each other kindly. Now when you are gone, they will start quarrelling and engage in loose talk."

The monk said: "If my living here makes you live at peace, that is good," and he stayed on there, and it was there that he eventually attained *Nibbāna*.

As for modern-day examples, an old monk in Myanmar (Burma), well-known for his *mettā*-practice, once recounted how a swarm of angry bees had attacked everyone around but him. The bee-hive had been disturbed and the bees flew out stinging everybody in sight. The monk said the people ran all over the place trying to flee from the bees but the bees did not sting him. In fact, he even walked right up to the bees' hive to find out what was the cause of their displeasure. A great number of angry bees flew out from the hive but still none stung the monk. The monk recounted the incident at a Dhamma talk as an encouragement to people to practise *mettā*.

On one occasion too when I was in Myanmar, I saw a sparrow fly towards a monk and land on his shoulder. There the bird rested a while before flying away. The monk at that time was doing intensive *mettā* meditation. He was standing and radiating *mettā* while waiting with other monks for the lunch gong to strike when the bird suddenly flew towards him.

Considering all these accounts one can appreciate the efficacy of *mettā*. It is not a practice to be thought lightly of.

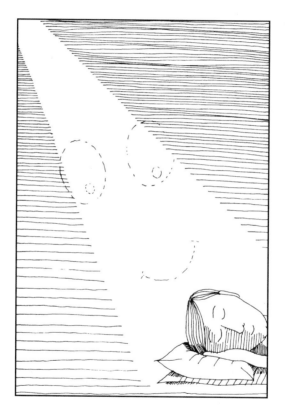

Devas protect him.

Devas (spirits) guard him: When one is dear to the *devas* it follows that they will protect one. An example is the earlier-mentioned case of the monks who were initially disturbed by *devas* while meditating in the forest. After winning over the *devas* by radiating *mettā*, the monks were further protected by the *devas* so that they all spent a safe and fruitful three months in the forest.

Nowadays, if *devas* should deign to protect us, we may perhaps uncannily escape dangers from time to time. Of course, our best protection and refuge is in truth and goodness. If we have done good we have actually nothing to fear, for good will inevitably beget good. There is the saying, too, that the Dhamma upholds those who uphold the Dhamma. Thus, if we live according to the Dhamma, we can be confident that the Dhamma will protect us. This is, in fact, the best protection.

So the practitioner of *mettā* and *Dhamma* is well protected. This is the true protection one should seek rather than charms and talismans whose efficacy is questionable. The Buddha thought poorly of such practices as resorting to charms and talismans and strongly discouraged any involvement in them.

 Fire, poison and weapons do not harm him: The *Visuddhimagga* mentions two incidents that occurred during the Buddha's time. One was the case of the laywoman devotee, Uttara. A woman who was jealous of Uttara had poured hot oil over her but she was not scalded in any way. To her, it was as if the hot oil was cold water. The other incident was that of a seven-year-old novice monk, Sankicca, who could not be injured by knives. Some robbers wanted to kill him to offer a sacrifice to their gods. But when they

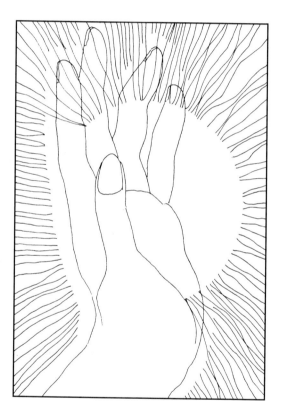

Fire, poison and weapons
do not harm him.

struck him with their swords, the weapons just bounced off. The blades could not cut him at all. Amazed and awed, the robbers fell at the feet of Sankicca, asked for forgiveness, and were converted to the Dhamma. There is also the story of a cow that was giving milk to her calf when a hunter threw a spear at her. The spear bounced off the cow simply because of the strength of her love for her calf. So mightily powerful is loving-kindness!

As for poison, my seventy-year-old teacher once recounted several of his own personal experiences. He had been practising *mettā* from his youth and as a young monk he was once pierced by the poisonous fin of a fish. He was trying to save fish from a pond that was drying up when he was accidentally injured by a struggling fish. His hand bled but he felt no pain nor did he feel any effect of the poison.

On another occasion he was trying to save a dog that had fallen into a well. He had managed to get the dog up near the top of the well and was putting his hand in to pull out the animal when it bit him. Apparently, the frightened animal was trying to grab hold of anything it could hang onto, and so sank his teeth into the hand that was actually going to pull him out. Still my teacher pulled up the dog and again, he said, he suffered no pain nor felt the effect of any poison although scars were left on his hand. Thus, although sometimes one may inadvertently be bitten, one's *mettā* can still protect one from pain or the effect of the poison.

His mind is easily concentrated: The mind of one who abides in loving-kindness is quickly concentrated; there is no sluggishness about it. This is because meditation helps

He is serene.

to collect the mind and purify it, making it one-pointed and wholesome. Consequently the habit of the mind to wander aimlessly and become distracted is curtailed. This results in better concentration in whatever one does. One should then be better able to do one's work well. Of course, with regard to meditation, concentration too will come more and more easily as one practises regularly.

 The expression of his face is serene: The meditator will have a serene countenance. This is a kind of beauty that comes from the heart. It is expressed in one's composure, serenity and radiance. A practitioner of *metta* needs no cosmetics. The beauty of *metta* is natural while that of cosmetics is artificial. Even if one is prettily made-up, one can still be ugly or repulsive if one has an unpleasant character or when anger flares up. That is why the Buddha stated that of all perfumes, such as sandalwood and jasmine, the perfume of virtue is by far the best. And furthermore, the fragrance of virtue, unlike ordinary perfumes, can blow against the wind.

Thus, if one can appreciate true beauty, the beauty that comes from the heart, one should cultivate loving-kindness and observe morality. Then, even if one may not possess fine physical features, one will acquire an intangible radiance and serenity that people will find attractive and lovable.

 He dies peacefully: All of us must die one day, though the way we live often shows that we are quite forgetful of this fact. Just as we must live well, we must die well. To live well means to live nobly, to uphold a high standard of integrity and

The perfume of virtue
blows against the wind.

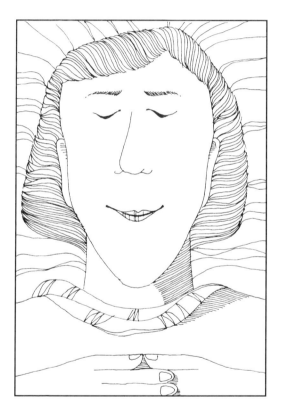

He dies peacefully.

morality. To die well means to die calmly, mindfully, peacefully—without fear or attachment, without tears or sorrow. A practitioner of *mettā* who lives with a heart full of love for living beings is one who lives well. He would live a moral life, having infused himself with this love and shown it in his words and deeds.

Consequently, when the time for death comes, he is ready. He is calm and peaceful. When he reflects on his life, he would have no regrets, having lived a life of love and morality. Thus the *Visuddhimagga* states that he passes away peacefully as if falling asleep.

In Buddhism, we are taught that it is important to die well because our next life is dependent on our last thought moment. If we die with a bad thought we will get a bad rebirth, if with a good thought a good rebirth. Dying with a mind trained in *mettā* means we are assured of a good destiny—one where we can continue our striving for *Nibbāna*—the end of all suffering.

 If he has not attained arahatship he will on death be reborn in the Brahma world: So a *mettā*-practitioner, if he has practised consistently and has attained the mundane *jhānas*, is assured of a rebirth in the plane of the *Brahma* gods. This is a fine heavenly plane where beings live with a fine material form enjoying mental bliss. Of course, if one can attain arahatship in this very life, it is best. Arahatship means the attainment of final *Nibbāna*, i.e. the end of all rebirth, the end of the cycle of birth and death, the cycle of suffering. To attain arahatship, however, one must practise *vipassanā* (insight) meditation. Thus we have emphasized earlier the need to balance *mettā* with *vipassanā* practice. Even with practice of *vipassanā*, it is not easy to attain arahatship in just one life. It is likely to take many, many more lives. Still one must try one's best and with mature *pāramis* (perfections from previous lives) one might well attain the goal in this life. After all, the Buddha has assured us in the *Mahā Satipaṭṭhāna Sutta* that a person who practises mindfulness meditation can attain arahatship between seven days and seven years, failing which he or she can attain anāgāmiship and the other lower levels of sainthood. Nevertheless, if one does not attain any level of sainthood, one can still be confident that with the support of one's *metta* practice, one is assured of a good rebirth that will enable one to continue the striving for arahatship.

Summary of
Benefits of Mettā

1 He sleeps easily.

2 He wakes up fresh like a flower opening.

3 He has no bad dreams.

4 He is dear to human beings.

5 He is dear to non-human beings.

6 *Devas* (spirits) guard him.

7 Fire, poison and weapons do not harm him.

8 His mind is easily concentrated.

9 The expression of his face is serene.

10 He dies peacefully.

11 If he has not attained arahatship he will
     on death be reborn in the *Brahma* world.

CURBING
ANGER
SPREADING
LOVE

 e have come to the end of our treatise "Curbing Anger, Spreading Love." We have explained at length the demerits of anger and how to check it through mindfulness and wise reflection. We have presented *mettā-bhāvanā,* i.e. loving-kindness meditation, as a counter-weapon to anger. We have elaborated on the many other benefits one can gain by practising *mettā.* We hope the reader, having come thus far, will put into practice the various suggestions and cultivate the radiation of loving-kindness. The approaches are all based on the Dhamma and we are confident that all those who try them will not be disappointed. To the contrary, when they see the improvement in their minds and the better control they will have over their lives, they will be positively delighted.

Ultimately, all of us need to live wisely with love and compassion. We need to do what we can for our fellow humans, guided by wisdom and compassion. And we start by creating the right temperament and attitudes that can lead us to that wisdom and compassion. When we become harmless, when we no longer flare up in anger but remain cool and self-composed, able to assess any situation calmly and respond with wisdom, we will be living well and happily. Finally, when all anger falls away and only wisdom and compassion guide our every action, we will have reached a happy abiding here and now, with no coming back here-after. That will be the end of suffering, the end of this long wandering in *saṁsāra*, from one birth to another, from suffering to suffering. Yes, when we reach full maturity in wisdom and compassion, the cycle of birth and death comes to a halt. And *Nibbāna*, the Buddha assures us, will then be ours. We may not know what exactly this *Nibbāna* is, but the Buddha has further assured us that in this state of *Nibbāna* all suffering ceases, and only peace, true peace, reigns. It is inviting, this message of hope, that *Nibbāna* can be attained in this life, the end of rebirth and suffering. All Buddhists have *Nibbāna* as their ultimate goal, and for those who may consider themselves sceptics, we suggest that they try walking the path of love and wisdom trodden by the Buddha and verify for themselves the Master's words. They certainly have nothing to lose and a priceless treasure to gain!

May all beings cultivate the path of love and wisdom culminating in the cessation of suffering and the realization of *Nibbāna*, the supreme happiness.

EPILOGUE

MAGIC MOUNTAIN

henever you are angry, freeze! Right there! Don't move! Don't do anything. Don't say anything—not even a word. Just stay absolutely still and quiet. Ignore completely the person or thing you are angry about or upset with. Then watch this mind and heart, watch the tension, the tightness, the pain, the choking feeling and sensation. Then watch some more and see as the poison, which is anger, cools down and fizzles away.

If that doesn't work, send your mind soaring away, flying through the clouds and alight on your favourite mountain retreat, amidst soothing greens, trees, shrubs and flowers—lovely pale blue hydrangeas, soft white roses or brilliant red or yellow, all your favourite colours. Breathe in the delightful fragrance and the pure mountain air, hear the melody of a mountain spring, step into the cool, refreshing waters, bathe under the wonderful showers of a gently cascading waterfall, watch the little fish swimming merrily in the pool, the butterflies flitting among the water lilies, listen to the frogs croaking and the birds chirping. All snug and cosy in the magic mountain resort of your mind, you'll feel as if you don't have a care in the world. (Truly, next to *Nibbāna,* this is bliss!)

Then look at the person you were angry with just a moment ago ... and smile — see how your anger has all melted away, as if into thin air. After bathing in the delightful cool waters on magic mountain, breathing in its superior air, basking in its many wondrous splendours, how could you be angry with him or her or anybody ever again?

Song of Love

May I be happy. May I preserve my happiness and live without enmity. May all beings be prosperous and happy. May they be of joyful mind, all beings that have life, be they feeble or strong, be they minute or vast, visible or invisible, near or afar, born or due to be born. May all beings be joyful.

Let no one deceive another, let none be harsh in speech, let none by anger or hatred wish ill to another. Even as a mother, at the risk of her life, watches over and protects her only child, so with a boundless heart of compassion I cherish all living beings, suffusing love over the entire world, above and all around without limit; thus I cultivate an infinite goodwill towards the whole world.

Standing or walking, sitting or lying down, during all my waking hours, I cherish the thought that this way of loving is the noblest in the world.

Thus shall I, by abandoning vain discussions and controversies, by walking righteously, be endowed with insight, subdue the longing for the pleasures of the senses, and never again know rebirth. May all sentient beings too, be fulfilled in the conditions leading to their attainment of *Nibbāna*. May all sentient beings escape the dangers of old age, disease and death. May all beings be liberated.

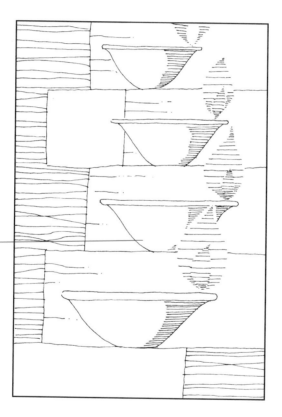

Like a little but steadily
glowing lamp, we can ignite
many other little lamps ....

THE BUDDHIST PUBLICATION SOCIETY

The BPS is an approved charity dedicated to making known the Teaching of the Buddha, which has a vital message for people of all creeds. Founded in 1958, the BPS has published a wide variety of books and booklets covering a great range of topics. Its publications include accurate annotated translations of the Buddha's discourses, standard reference works, as well as original contemporary expositions of Buddhist thought and practice. These works present Buddhism as it truly is—a dynamic force which has influenced receptive minds for the past 2500 years and is still as relevant today as it was when it first arose. A full list of our publications will be sent upon request. Write to:

The Hony. Secretary
Buddhist Publication Society
P.O. Box 61
54, Sangharaja Mawatha
Kandy • Sri Lanka